Books should be returned or renewed by the last
date above. Renew by phone **03000 41 31 31** or
online *www.kent.gov.uk/libs*

Pebble® Plus

DINOSAURS

STEGOSAURUS

by Tammy Gagne

raintree
a Capstone company — publishers for children

Raintree is an imprint of Capstone Global Library Limited, a company
incorporated in England and Wales having its registered office at 264
Banbury Road, Oxford, OX2 7DY – Registered company number: 6695582

www.raintree.co.uk
myorders@raintree.co.uk

Edited by Hank Musolf
Designed by Charmaine Whitman
Picture research by Kelly Garvin
Production by Laura Manthe
Illustrated by Jon Hughes/Capstone Press
Originated by Capstone Global Library Ltd
Printed and bound in India

ISBN 978 1 4747 5223 7
22 21 20 19 18
10 9 8 7 6 5 4 3 2 1

British Library Cataloguing in Publication Data
A full catalogue record for this book is available from the British Library.

Design elements: Shutterstock/Krasovski Dmitri

Contents

Meet the stegosaurus

The stegosaurus was not the biggest or the smallest dinosaur. It was about 9 metres (30 feet) long. This is about the size of a single-decker bus.

The stegosaurus weighed more than 1,587 kilograms (3,500 pounds). It had bony plates down its back. They made this species look bigger.

The stegosaurus had a small head. Its brain was about the size of a hot dog! Scientists do not think the stegosaurus was very clever.

Plant eaters

The stegosaurus had a beak like a bird. It had round teeth shaped like pegs. But the dinosaur had no front teeth.

The stegosaurus was a herbivore. It ate small plants with its weak jaws. Because it had short legs, the stegosaurus fed on plants on the ground.

Stegosaurus bones

The stegosaurus lived about 150 million years ago.

This species of dinosaur lived in North America, Europe, Asia and Africa.

Scientists have found bones of about 80 stegosauruses in the United States. This species probably travelled in herds. These groups had both young and old dinosaurs.

Defending itself

The stegosaurus could not outrun predators. Short legs made the dinosaur slow. It used its tail to fight off attackers.

The stegosaurus had long spikes on its tail. Some spikes were 1.2 metres (4 feet) long. Other dinosaur bones have been found with marks from these spikes.

Glossary

herbivore animal that only eats plants

herd group of animals that live and move together

predator animal that hunts other animals for food

scientist person who studies the way the world works

skeleton bones of an animal

species group of animals with similar features

Read more

Dinosaurs (Usborne Beginners), Stephanie Turnbull
(Usborne Publishing Ltd, 2006)

Dinosaurs: a children's encyclopedia,
DK (DK Children, 2011)

World's Dumbest Dinosaurs (Extreme Dinosaurs),
Rupert Matthews (Raintree, 2012)

Websites

www.bbc.co.uk/cbeebies/curations/dinosaur-facts

www.dkfindout.com/uk/dinosaurs-and-prehistoric-life/
dinosaurs/inside-stegosaurus/

Comprehension questions

1. Do you think other dinosaurs feared the stegosaurus? Why or why not?

2. How do you think scientists know that both older and younger stegosauruses lived in the same herds?

3. Do you think the stegosaurus could have won fights against predators by biting them? Explain your answer.

Index